JOANNA HIGA

PRETEND NO MORE

MY HEALING PROCESS FROM DOMESTIC VIOLENCE

Published in the United States of America
Brilliant Books Literary
137 Forest Park Lane Thomasville
North Carolina 27360 USA

ISBN:
Paperback: 979-8-88945-473-1
Ebook: 979-8-88945-474-8

I dedicate this book to my sons Rahula, Ananda, and Martin.
I survived for you and because of you. This book is also dedicated to all
the people who supported, helped and encouraged me.

INTRODUCTION

It's been said that mental and emotional abuse are worse than physical abuse. From my experience, the mental and emotional abuse inevitably accompanied the physical. I am recovering from the trauma and damage of domestic violence. This book of poetry and sketches is my healing process. I am by no means even halfway healed but if I had not turned my reflective writing into a creative process, using poetic form and sketches, I would have not healed as much as I have thus far. This creative process has probably saved me from being enticed into unhealthy vices like drugs and alcohol. There's no doubt that I am healing. I now experience more positive days than negative ones. But I know I have a long way to go. I can be having a really positive day, when it can go sour and bitter in an instant. One morning on my way to work, I happened to stop behind a car with a bumper sticker that read, "THERE'S NO EXCUSE FOR DOMESTIC VIOLENCE." I burst into tears and cried all the way to work. I want to experience less and less of these negative days. My heart aches to write happy poetry instead of angry ones. It is my hope that this book will empower people to use their courage to get out of their abusive relationship. Also, it is my hope that this book will wake up those who are raising hateful, angry, and unruly children. Some people may take offense to the strong language used in my writing but that's okay. I had a long inner struggle concerning my use of foul language. This was especially a concern because I am a school teacher who emphasizes character education and the importance of practicing good manners and social skills. I decided against changing the language because changing it would have meant losing my voice and weakening its effectiveness. Afterall, those words came from my angry heart, as a part of my healing process. In other words, I had to "Keep it real."

Falling

I am running from my shadow,
I come to a cliff, the shadow is gaining,
Should I jump? I can't see the bottom,
I turn around to see the shadow, a few steps behind,
I finally make up my mind to jump.
I am falling, falling, falling to my doom,
I close my eyes so I won't have to see.

It has been a long time, and I'm still falling,
I open my eyes, only to see,
The color my eyes saw when my eyes were closed…pitch black.
What is going on? Is this fall ever going to end?
Will the rest of my life be spent falling? Until I die?

I hear my self praying.
Praying for my life,
Praying for my future.
I plead, "Please don't let me die this way,
I will change my life to go up, not down,
So please, don't let me die this way."

I wait and wait for the answers to my prayer,
Waiting for what seems to be years.
All of a sudden, there is light.
I look down to see the ground, and I see the shadow…
The shadow that was chasing me before.
That same shadow sticks out its arms,
It catches me and embraces me.

By Martin Hall
05.19.01

(5) feeling forsaken
(4) broken spirit
(3) shattered faith
(2) bitter
(1) lost
(2) frightened
(3) must break free
(4) time to go home
(5) mommy will be there

08.29.01

Pour down the chili sauce
To blast away the numbness
Show who's the boss
And stop all the b.s.

01.17.02

The House of Pain and Healing

The punished come here
Even the blameless come too
The karma receivers, the pity seekers
The lesson learners, the energy suckers
We all assemble here, in fear
At the house of pain and healing.

You feel hopeful one day
The plan just might work
You feel hopeless the next day
The plan might make things worse
Confused and scared
You share and console
You tell your story over and over
You wear yourself out
You don't want to tell it anymore

You want to go home
You want to stay
You want to feel safe
And you want to heal
But it's hard to heal
When there's so much pain
And the hotline rings
Another arrival
Another intake
And more pain
01.21.09

Abuse A – Z

angel away
bones bruised
courage crushed
demons deadly
ego empty
face fucked-up
grief gigantic
insight icy
jaw jarred
ki killed
life leaving
mind murky
navel numb
optimism over
pain perfumed
quietness quivering
righteousness ripped
sight shrinking
taste tainted
understanding useless
voice vaporized
will wounded
x-ray xd
yearnings yielded
zeal zero

02.07.02

My parents are fucking me up
Like their parents did them
Please help me
Please give me new parents.
Please?

02.08.02

Serene Sunday?
Hell no!
Not in this house
Souls sling shit on Sundays
What a shame
What a sacrilege

02.12.02

Das right
Shut da fuck up
I no mo time to read you one book
I gotta smoke one cigarette and joke around wit Aunty
Now go play wit your braddah
I said go you fucka
Shit man, dese fuckin' kids stay driving me crazy
What?
You stay whining again?
Shit!
I no mo time to play truck wit you
Go play wit your braddah
I like smoke one cigarette and play around wit Aunty
Now go play and no forget to clean up da fuckin' mess afta
You heard?
Shut up I said
Shut your fuckin' mout
I no mo time to tell you one story
I make time to smoke one cig and talk story with Aunty
No go inside and watch da video Aunty wen bring
You said you like watch, so go watch
Yeah, it's da one wit planny sex and violence
Hurry up...stay on already
No bada me
And no mess up da fuckin' couch bcfo I give you one crack
I jus wen fix um
I like slap da fuckin' shit out of dem kids
Tank God for des cigs
And tank God I get some fun talking wit you Girlfriend
Or I swear I don know what da fuck I would do to dem fuckin' kids

02.12.02

Sometimes,
I wish I had done
All the things
He accused me of doing.

At least then,
I could have
Sweet memories
To replace
All the
Bitter ones.

02.14.02

Mind everybody else's business
So I don't have to mind my own.
Be nosey about theirs
To escape mine.

02.15.02

Wow!
You're good at finding fault
With her parenting.
You're good at observing.
But why does it bother you so much
When you stay parenting the same fuckin' way?

02.15.02

How many holes
must I punch
in the walls
before they notice me?

How many times in a day
must I scream
at my kid
that he's fuckin' stupid
before they hear me?

How many bruises
must I put on my kid's arms
before they notice
how pretty my hands are?

How many black eyes
must I give my kid
before they see
how gorgeous my eyes are?

What the hell must I do
so they'll take my kid
away from me?

02.19.02

Don't borrow anything from anyone
They'll swear you never returned it
Watch your things
Watch your back
Be yourself
But be cautious

03.10.02

During the time of his violent outbursts,
I had the need to watch kung fu movies;
Especially ones with women warriors,
As if I could draw strength from them,
As if I could draw courage from them,
As if their warrior spirit would possess me;
How I wished for guts to fight back,
Instead of just blocking the blows.
I played it in my head so many times,
But it never happened.
Finally however,
Another spirit possessed me
It told me to RUN LIKE HELL!
And I did!

03.14.02

Today's society
Cell phone mania
Causing near crack-ups
Minding the phone
Instead of the road
B.S.ing
Gossiping
Checking up on a spouse's whereabouts
So many people passing by
See me taking blows
Why won't they use their cells
Please someone…
Call 911
Don't turn your head away
Don't pretend not to see
It's d.v. in your face.
Now's the time to be a busybody
Please help me.
Believe me,
I understand.
I used to be that way
And that's why I'm mad as hell
Because I too,
would have turned the other way.

11.15.02

An event
A glimpse
A thought
Seemingly insignificant
Triggers an angry memory
Leaving a bitter aftertaste
Lingering and lingering
Making me feel yucky
For the rest of the day

12.02.02

An acquaintance asked "You still single?"
Hell yeah!
No more interrogations and accusations
No more ordering around
No more blaming and put-downs
No more terror and trauma
No more damage
You think I miss any of that?
Hell no!
You think I want to give up this freedom?
Hell no!
And anyway…
I'm an angry witch
A frickin' bitter bitch
With no more sweetness to offer
So yeah…
I'm still single

12.19.02

A tea kettle is me
And I am boiling mad.
I'm steamed and hot
And I feel so bad.

The heat is rising
The pressure is building.
I say with a shout
"Hurry and pour it all out!"

02.12.03

The donation room warden
Volunteers to organize the room
Keeps a watchful eye
Of what comes in
And what goes out
And who took what
Oh and of course
Gets first crack as the gold comes in
Who will be the next donation room warden when she leaves?

03.20.03

Poor Penny
Your last name ought to be Pitiful
No, Pitiful should come first
Pitiful Penny
It's always about you, isn't it?
How many people has it been
Trying to pick you up
Giving you a kick in the pants
To get you out of the mud
Too many
How many people have handed you a rope
To pull you out from the deep
Too, too many
You cry and complain that you can't get your son back
And yet you won't do what it takes to get him back
You say you can't
You say it's too hard
Okay then, give up
And be happy he's getting the love and care he needs
We're tired of hearing your sorry story
So you tell someone else
And someone else
And someone else
First they pity you
Then they get tired
Then they get sick of the sight of you
Because you suck their energy
You're a sucker Penny
Pitiful Suckin' Penny
04.06.03

Terror, for a second, grips me
Every time I see a car that looks like his.

05.12.03

Ace One Taxi
My life saver
To the safe house you took me, more than once
Compassionate drivers
Empathetic drivers
Sensitive drivers
Very professional
Know when and how to chat
Know when to stay aloof
Know when to show silent support
You truly are Ace One
Thank you for your service
Thank you

05.14.03

Turn up the music
Drown out the noise in my head
Drink up the brew boiling hot
Warm my icy heart
Drop ten sugar cubes in a cup of coffee
Soften the bitter taste
Write poem after poem like a lunatic
Quell the rage running through my veins
NO!
Numb NOT my senses
Let me feel what I need to feel
Let me say what I need to say
Let me hate who I need to hate
Just let me be

07.04.03

Women:
Be careful when you utter these words in the heat of the moment:
"Control me"

Women:
Be careful when he asks you in the heat of the moment:
"Aren't you my Baby?"

Women:
Take care how you respond when he says in the heat of the moment:
"You belong to me"

07.07.03

I had to know why
I knew I didn't deserve this
Is it karma
Is it punishment
Is it a lesson
Is it the stars
Tell me why
I need to know
Then I heard someone say
There doesn't have to be a why
Shit just happens
I can live with that explanation
For now

07.09.03

Be whole first
Then share yourself

Be secure in who you are
Then give of yourself

Don't let him kill your identity
Be you
And if he can't accept you
Get rid of him

10.26.03

In each experience
Is a hidden treasure

11.04.03

CLOSING

thank you for taking the time to read my book. If you are in an abusive relationship, it is my hope that this book will help you draw upon the courage which lies within you. And if you are fortunate to not experience violence in your life, I hope this book will awaken the spirit of empathy that lies within you. Please don't ignore the signs of domestic violence.

My healing process is still in progress. I am yet dealing with my anger and resentment. Fortunately, I have found a creative way of releasing my negative energy. By turning my reflections into poetry and by keeping a sketchbook journal, I am able to slowly, but surely heal. I have also found another way to work out my anger. Work. Work is my medicine. Sometimes, I feel like Wonder Woman, working long hours, seven days a week and sleeping only a few hours every night. For me, doing jobs that require physical energy is key. Exerting great physical energy is having a therapeutic effect on me. Sometimes I shock myself with the incredible amount of strength and energy I possess. I know that it is not only anger that is driving me, but it is also my need of running from the fear of falling into a deep depression. That's it! I just made a self-discovery! Now I know why I'm almost tirelessly going from one workplace to the other and working like some crazed person, not being able to slow down. There's one more thing…I need to be around people right now. Being around fun co-workers is brightening my life. When I'm in contact with fun and positive people, I feel my spirit getting lighter and livelier. So this is where I'm at. I have a ways to go but I'll surely get there, with my sanity intact.

So once again, thank you for reading my book. By doing so, you have helped me in my healing process and progress. And hopefully, my words will help others in similar or worse situations.

ABOUT THE AUTHOR

Joanna's ultimate goal is to write and illustrate children's books. But before she can complete the two children's books that she's been working on, Joanna decided that this book of reflective poetry and sketches about her recovery from domestic abuse needed first priority. By sharing her story through poems and sketches, she hopes to inspire others in similar situations to use a creative process of healing.